MEMORIES OF MUM
and some random stuff too

A poetry book by M.D Head

MUM

I sit here thinking,
alone with my thoughts,
how you used to be,
how you enjoyed your walks,
a tear escapes my eye.

Is it a tear of regret?
Or just emotional unrest?
Could I have done more?
Should I try to forget?

I tried so very hard,
to make life easy for you,
I tried so hard it hurt,
sometimes though I wonder,
If you already knew,
what it was you heard?

You were always there for me,
always the first to reassure,
you never stopped believing in me,
gave me confidence,
when I was unsure.

If I think about you,
a little too long,
my tears will fall once more,
so I say a short prayer,
knowing your memory,
will stay forever more.

ITS OKAY TO FALL ASLEEP

Remember when we visited you,
My sister and I trying not to cry,
The way you would strain,
to keep your eyes open,
though we reassured you,
Its okay to fall asleep.

Once when we visited,
You looked so peaceful,
No pain could be seen,
Upon your face,

All we could hear,
Was your faint breathing,
It was the loudest noise,
Within the place.

All these people,
Coming to and thro,
Family, friends and staff,
Who sometimes would feel,
the wrath of your tongue,
Or on occasion making them laugh.

Often we would think,
When you tried to drink,
If there was more,
we could of done,
that maybe we could try,
One day to get you in the sun.

Next time there's a nice day,
I will think of you mum,
The way you would sit in your chair,
Chatting away with the family,
Cigarette in hand,
With no care.

ASHTRAYS AND DVDS

The ashtray she one used,
Is empty now,
No more will it feel the tap,
When the ash is flicked,
At times your ciggy would snap.

I remember us watching dvds,
Be it rock n roll or musicals,
The way you would sing along,
Often singing the wrong words.

Elvis was our favourite,
We would often recall,
the way he would perform,
his command of all.

How many times,
did we watch the same DVD,
even though we had seen it before,
or watch a tv show unfamiliar to us,
i would end up watching,
while you would snore.

RED COWBOY BOOTS

I got them mum,
those red cowboy boots,
the ones I showed you,
the other day..

They fit so well,
they really rock,
I'm going to wear them,
funeral day.

You always said,
you liked it,
When cowboy boots,
I would wear.

So I shall wear them,
In your honour,
Because you liked them,
so let them stare.

SHADOW DREAMS

I dream of a face,
Not always clear to me,
Not always easy to see.

I feel the presence,
Its strong and clear,
I can almost touch it,
Though I never seem,
to get that near.

She's with me,
when I'm alone,
in a memory,
Like a home.

I wish at times,
the dream would last,
that the shadows would clear,
somehow maybe,
rearrange our past.

Sometimes I cry,
At times in sadness,
At times with joy,
and I remember,
the happy times,
when we would laugh,
My mum and her boy.

I miss you mum,
I will every day,
sometimes I will grieve,
maybe I will pray.

I know your at peace now,
your no longer in pain,
I will see you someday soon,
and we'll laugh and joke again.

Death

You say when it happens,
Your be prepared,
You reckon that,
You won't be scared.

You spend hours in conversation,
discussing the situation,
You listen and try to understand,
the doctors evaluation.

Funeral arranging,
is always hard,
Knowing there will always be,
someone who finds it hard.

The choices you will make,
can be the hardest you take,
You know someone,
always will be put out.

Sometimes people forget,
When sorting things out,
What it is,
The day is about.

RECOGNITION

Hey mum,
do you remember,
when I started being noticed,
by nearly everyone,
just after I did my modelling,
in your favourite newspaper,
the Sun.

First of all,
we just played it cool,
I tried to be totally unfazed,
though after a while,
I got used to it,
I secretly relished those days.

You always tried to keep,
my feet firmly on the ground,
even when I signed autographs,
for people all around.

You installed in me the fact,
that fame was just a bonus,
a recognition of hard work,
you told me never to judge,
a book by its cover,
that everyone deserves respect,
on this earth.

I remember growing up,
listening to different genres of music,
you telling me I should try to appreciate,
all artists and their music.

You always said it was important,
to experience all aspects of showbiz,
to try to learn from all those involved,
traits and talents for longevity to prevail.

I always remember what you told me,
about Tommy Steele,
how he started as a rock n roller,
who then became a musical theatre star,
meaning his career,
would last that much longer.

Your experience in the 'Industry',
was always a help to me.
your tales about the down side,
would be kept in my mind constantly.

One day mum I will own a mansion,
just like Elvis did and call it Valerie.
My ego though will have to,
have my initials on the gates,
so everyone knows its owned by me.

Jesus!!!

I saw Jesus running,
He was on the sand,
There were wings on his back,
He was in a strange land.

He was running to something,
of which I don't know,
It was something mechanical,
But exactly what I don't know.

A lady appeared,
she began to laugh,
Saying she could remember,
Watching it once before.

I told her,
we could watch it together,
She smiled and said okay,
Then I woke up with a smile,
Ready for a new day.

MY FIRST BOOK

I remember,
writing my very first book,
showing it to my mum,
she read a chapter every night,
that would make,
her feel less glum.

As the weeks went by,
I would try not to cry,
as I saw her struggle to get by,
I would read it to her,
and often would see,
a glint appear,
in her eye.

Sometimes I wish,
I could write a story,
where the happy ending,
in real life would come true,
but this 'is' real life,
and in this world,
the strongest of wishes,
never do.

Death

You say when it happens,
Your be prepared,
You reckon that,
You won't be scared.

You spend hours in conversation,
discussing the situation,
You listen and try to understand,
the doctors evaluation.

Funeral arranging,
is always hard,
Knowing there will always be,
someone who finds it hard.

The choices you will make,
can be the hardest you take,
You know someone,
always will be put out.

Sometimes people forget,
When sorting things out,
What it is,
The day is about.

"THE RANDOM STUFF"

ME

When you see me,
on the cover of a book,
for just an instant,
what do you see.

Do you see a face,
of a someone,
you think you know,
who unlike you,
refused to just 'be'.

Does it surprise you,
finding my book,
in your local shop,
where you go,
to spend your money.

Are you shocked,
amused at what you see,
this face you used to call "funny"
that face,
you tried to embarrass,
by calling silly names.

That face that now,
looks down on you,
as something,
that belongs,
in the drains.

I always find it amusing,
when I think,
of people from school,
the ones who thought,
they would always be,
that are now,
simply nothing at all.

CHOCOLATE BOOK TOWER

I find myself in a tower,
within a castle,
within a dream.
I'm walking up steps,
And hearing a stream.

Where these steps lead,
I don't really know,
but they're made out of books,
made with chocolate,
and they glow.

The temperature I feel,
is becoming quite warm,
making me feel clammy,
within the clothes,
that adorn.

As I reach the top,
I see a door,
that just will not open,
the stairs are now,
beginning to melt,
yet the door,
still will not open.

I stand on the edge,
of the last chocolate step,
which I see,
is melting away,
the door still won't budge,
as I try one more shove,
as my surroundings,
Slowly fade away.

I feel my senses cry out,
as all at once I awake,
confused as to what,
the dream meant as I shake.

SHARKS AND STRANGE CREATURES

I stood on a cliff,
the sky was grey,
the wind was cold,
It was an okay day.

I looked down at the sea,
there was something within,
that seemed quite familiar,
as well as a surprise and shocking.

It was a shark just swimming,
beneath the waves,
that had these strange beings,
that were like drawings,
I had seen in caves.

As the shark swam along,
the small creatures were attached,
they were actually living on the shark,
as I saw another hatch.

Their bodies were small,
With fish like features,
almost looking human,
apart from the gills,
And webbed fingers.

The shark was a great white,
with coal black eyes,
the creatures would all shout,
When out the water it would rise.

The shark then dived,
far beneath the surface,
never to be seen again,
and the caves I saw the pictures in,
my mind was unable to retain.

TRAFFIC JAM

Is there anything,
quite so frustrating,
as being stuck,
in a cue,
of traffic,
when you know,
the culprit,
is not you.

You sit there,
twiddling your fingers,
deliberating,
what you can do,
turn the engine off,
listen to some music,
to amuse just you.

When you eventually,
find something,
you might be able to do,
the traffic starts flowing again,
car horns now,
aimed at you.

You don't let yourself react,
you just breath slowly,
in........then........out,
keeping yourself calm,
knowing that to onlookers,
your mind has gone out!!!

AUTOMATED

So I'm using,
an automated system,
because it's what you do,
to make life easier,
for the public,
that's me and you.

The automated system,
doesn't always work,
It puts you through,
to a real person,
who makes you feel,
like a 'berk'.

The person asks you,
What it is they can help,
you with today,
and you can almost,
hear them sigh,
as you prepare to say.

You explain the situation,
the system has put you in,
then you cry a little,
Inside your head,
knowing the real person,
Is listening to you,
wearing a grin.

The automated system,
is great when it works,
but every now and again,
makes people feel,
like complete berks.

MALE ADOLESCENCES ADDRESSE
(In a way)

I THINK I'M A WEREWOLF
It started in my teens,
when I became aware,
that slowly my body,
was growing hair,
EVERY WHERE .

At first my face,
became quite furry,
then appeared on my chest,
thick and curly.

At night I would itch,
where I hadn't before,
for there was hair
'down there' too.

I asked my parents,
to explain my dilemma,
Laughing, they just said
"Us too."

They told me I was changing,
into one of them,
an adult,
but not to worry,
its quite normal too.

SCARLET FIELDS

The General sends his troops,
to fight another bloody war,
human pawns doing battle,
like so many did before.

Some will survive,
countless will fall,
in order to achieve,
peace for all.

At the end of the battle,
a strange silence can be heard,
the ones still standing,
Seem to utter no word.

For when all shots,
have been fired,
every blade coloured red,
the good and the bad,
are no different when dead.

THE OLD FRIEND

You know what you did,
that day in June,
when your betrothed,
was out shopping,
in the afternoon.

The old friend you caught up with,
you hadn't seen since school,
who certainly had changed,
now looking sexy and cool.

You couldn't believe it,
this vision that sat before you,
making you laugh,
like your betrothed would used to do.

You ordered some drinks,
then your friend ordered more,
You went back to theirs for coffee,
where you laughed and drunk more.

At the end of the evening,
you bid the friend goodnight,
then she pulls you towards her,
Saying why call it a night.

The next day you awake,
with a throbbing head,
you curse yourself for drinking,
saying your not a teenager anymore.

You stretch out your arms,
giving such a big yawn,
then you see the old friend,
naked as the day she was born.

Why did you do it,
is it really that hard,
to stay faithful,
to someone special,
even when times feel hard.

You know your betrothed
has got to be told,
for you know,
thats the right thing to do.

So you quietly leave,
your old friend to sleep,
looking so relaxed and content,
just like she should be for unlike you,
she has no reasons to repent.

You make your way home,
walking through the door,
betrothed is waiting to greet you,
she tells you how worried,
she has been all night,
that something bad,
might have happened to you.

Taking a deep breath,
you hear yourself say,
in your head what you know,
you should say.

As the words leave,
your mouth though,
what your actually saying,
is a complete and utter lie.

Your live with the guilt,
till the day you die,
you would hate,
to see her cry.

MY CHILDHOOD TOYS

I can remember,
waking up on Christmas Day,
to see what Santa had brought.
seeing piles of presents,
Stacked up high,
around a brand new tree.
we had bought.

There were action figures,
from my favourite shows,
some were bionic too,
there were space ships,
ray guns and robots as-well,
that would light up in colours,
from orange to blue.

Radio control cars,
we're an absolute must,
going so fast,
they would kick up dust.

There were figures,
and vehicles from movies,
you just had to have,
there was always one or two,
you could never get.

Sometimes my toys were robots,
that could transform into cars,
or planes and other things,
Sometimes I had figures,
that would ride large animals,
like tigers or panthers or horses.

TREES

If trees were people,
do you think,
they would say,
"Stop cutting us down."
as the world wastes away.

Some trees,
could tell stories,
about when they,
were first planted,
they could tell you,
how life was back then.

Can you imagine,
what the world was like,
when your grandpa,
would ride his bike,
to places new and afar.

When an inside toilet,
meant you were special,
or your family were rich,
if you owned a car.

Over the years,
things will change,
which is the way,
it's supposed to be,
certain things though,
must stay the same,
like the ever growing tree.

CLAM

I used to be a man,
though now I am a clam,
I live under the water,
and hang out with Mr Merman.

THE STALLION
I saw it once when riding,
I was only very young,
this horse,
that almost looked majestic,
just running free and having fun.

I rode my horse,
to the same spot,
the very next day,
after school,
there he was, the
eyes aflame,
powerful,strong and tall.

His coat was the darkest,
glossiest black,
steam would be released,
through flaring nostrils.

When he ran,
it was like,
he was running on air,
his mane,
was the shiniest of hair.

I came back the next day,
to watch the stallion,
sadly he was not there,
though now and again,
I can hear his roar,
coming from out of no where.

THE HOUSE

There were rumours,
stories and happenings,
involving it.

Some people say,
It's been there forever,
creepy looking,
night and day,
like a corpse,
that won't decay.

Those that enter,
rarely come out,
for the house is evil,
its victims,
scream and shout.

An old man,
once told us a story,
about when he,
was just a boy.
It was about a time,
he overthrew his best toy.

He had thrown his ball,
just a little too far,
the memory,
we could see,
made his mind jar

ECZEMA

What is it about Eczema,
that allergic annoyance,
that never goes away.

You scratch and scratch,
till the itch goes away,
though your left,
with a bloody mess,
the very next day.

Your skin is covered,
with dry wounds that weep,
that you self inflicted,
last night in your sleep.

When your stressed about stuff,
its even worse than usual,
you find your fingernails,
are filled with dry blood.

Your bed is covered,
in pieces of torn skin,
that you know the next day,
Will be replaced with fresh skin.

Its an awful allergy,
when people don't understand,
why there's pieces of skin,
torn away from your hand.

When its hot its the worse,
as sweating makes you itch,
then before you know it,
your healed wounds,
are torn open like a loose stitch

All you can do is perceiver,
keep applying the lotions,
sometime white or clear,
diligence they say is the key.

Until a cure to this allergy,
can really be found,
I will keep trying,
not to scratch,
making that scraping sound.

CLOCKS

There's something reassuring,
in a very simple way,
how after that first tiny tick,
a tock will be along the way.

You see there are so many,
clocks around the globe,
that light up, play music,
or talk to you.

The simple sound,
of that resounding tick,
followed with an echoey tock,
is just enough to let you know,
what stays the same,
is the sound of a clock

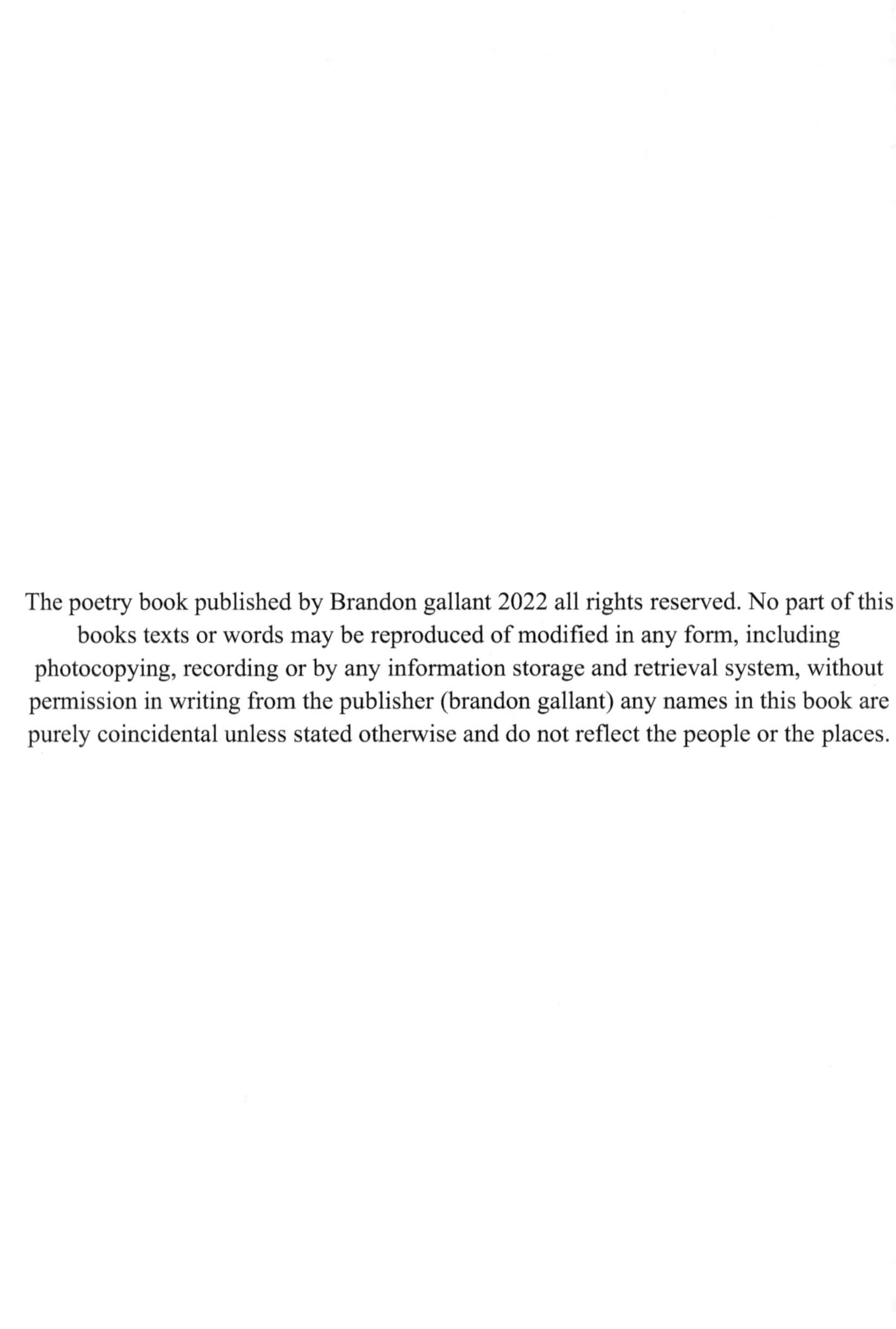

www.ingramcontent.com/pod-product-compliance
Lightning Source LLC
Chambersburg PA
CBHW051941150726
47999CB00006B/2321